Mr. Cricket
Finds a Friend

Patricia R. Kelly and Annette Zuidland

Illustrated by Steve Pileggi

Dominie Press, Inc.

Publisher: Raymond Yuen
Series Editor: Stanley L. Swartz
Consultant: Adria F. Klein
Editor: Bob Rowland
Designers: Lois Stanfield and Vincent Mao
Illustrator: Steve Pileggi

First published 1995
New Edition © 2001 Dominie Press, Inc.

All rights reserved. No part of this publication may be reproduced or transmitted in any form or by any means without permission in writing from the publisher. Reproduction of any part of this book, through photocopy, recording, or any electronic or mechanical retrieval system, without the written permission of the publisher, is an infringement of the copyright law.

Published by:

Dominie Press, Inc.

1949 Kellogg Avenue
Carlsbad, California 92008 USA

www.dominie.com

ISBN 1-56270-372-2

Printed in Singapore by PH Productions Pte Ltd
1 2 3 4 5 6 PH 03 02 01

ITP

It was spring.

Mr. Cricket was sad
in his new home.

He was safe and warm,
but he was too lonely
to sing.

Mr. Cricket set out to find a friend.

He crawled under the big door, hopped down the steps, and jumped into the yard.

He met some ants in the grass.

They were too busy working to talk.

He hopped into the bushes
and met a caterpillar
on a leaf.

He was too busy eating to talk.

He hopped into the garden
and saw a bee
on a flower.

She was too busy buzzing to talk.

He hopped onto a log
and saw another cricket.

She was not too busy to talk.

Mr. Cricket asked her to be his friend, and she said yes.

He was so happy,
he started to sing.